N
Co

enew

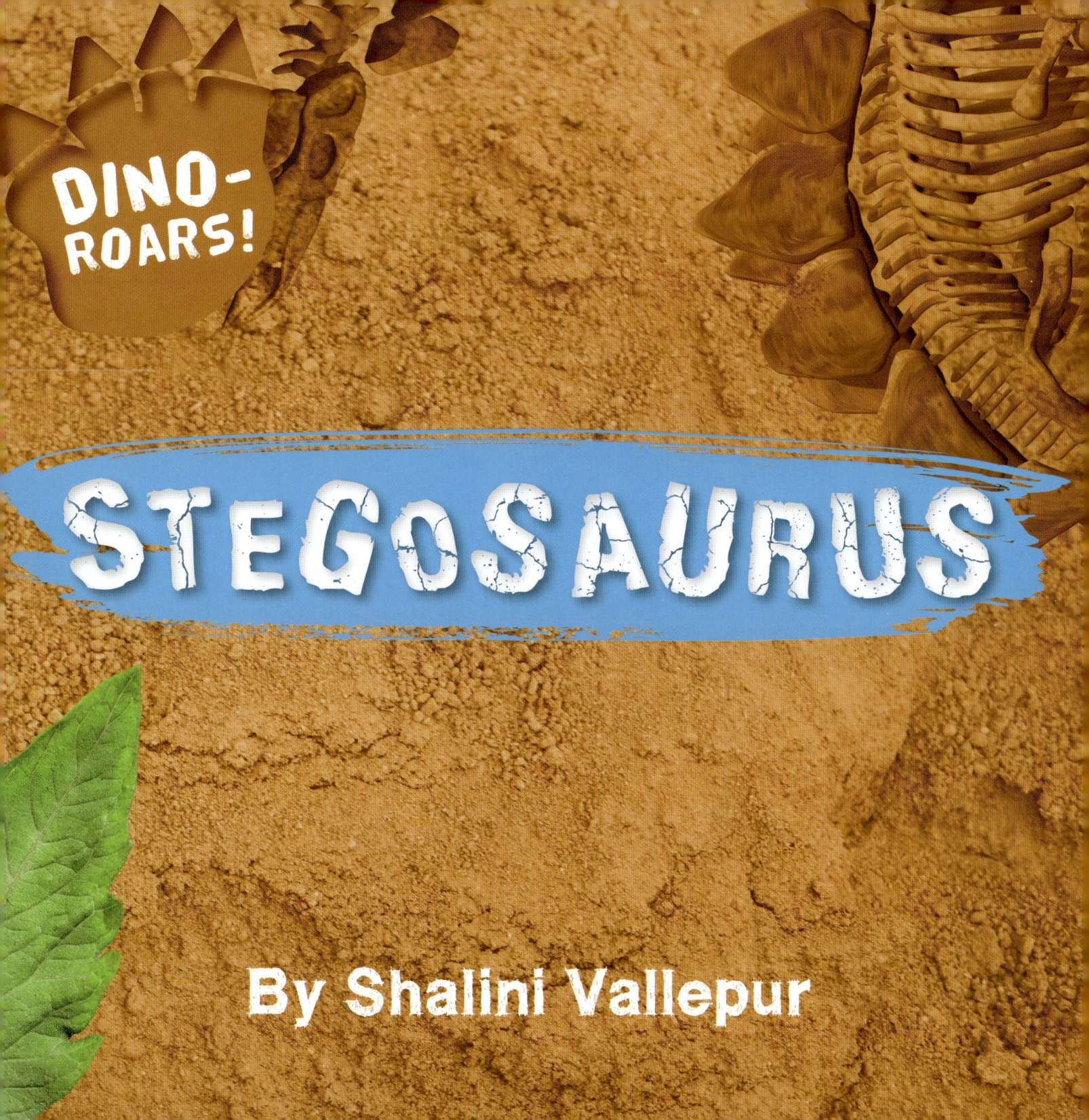

DINO-ROARS!

STEGOSAURUS

By Shalini Vallepur

BookLife
PUBLISHING

©2019
BookLife Publishing Ltd.
King's Lynn
Norfolk PE30 4LS

A catalogue record for this book is available from the British Library.

ISBN: 978-1-78637-737-1

Written by:
Shalini Vallepur

Edited by:
Madeline Tyler

Designed by:
Danielle Jones

All facts, statistics, web addresses and URLs in this book were verified as valid and accurate at time of writing. No responsibility for any changes to external websites or references can be accepted by either the author or publisher.

Photocredits:
Images are courtesy of Shutterstock.com.
With thanks to Getty Images, Thinkstock Photo and iStockphoto.

Front Cover - Luis Louro 2 - AKKHARAT JARUSILAWONG. 4 - paleontologist natural, Luis Louro. 5 - Javier Crespo, anmbph, Vadym Zaitsev, studiovin, BlackSTAR-FOTOGRAFiE. 6 - Nadezda Murmakova, YuRi Photolife. 7 - Elnur. 8 – Michael Rosskothen. 9 - Herschel Hoffmeyer. 10 - UnknownUnknown author [Public domain], via Wikimedia Commons, Othniel Charles Marsh, uploaded by Firsfron & modified by anetode [Public domain], via Wikimedia Commons, udovichenko. 11 - IR Stone. 12 - WindVector. 13 - Lopolo, achiaos, Artush. 14 - Vasilyev Alexandr. 15 - sebra, Daderot [CC0], from Wikimedia Commons, 5 second Studio. 16 - Freer. 17 - GermanOle [GFDL (http://www.gnu.org/copyleft/fdl.html) or CC BY-SA 3.0 (https://creativecommons.org/licenses/by-sa/3.0)], from Wikimedia Commons. 18 - Susannah Maidment et al. & Natural History Museum, London [CC BY 4.0 (https://creativecommons.org/licenses/by/4.0)], via Wikimedia Commons. 19 - Valentyna Chukhlyebova, AKKHARAT JARUSILAWONG. 20 - Lopolo, Hedzun Vasyl, Suwat wongkham. 22 - kamomeen. 23 - Luis Louro, Linda Bucklin.

CONTENTS

Words that look like **this** can be found in the glossary on page 24.

WELCOME TO THE DINO-TREK!

Check out page six to learn all about dinosaur fossils!

Get ready to see some dinosaurs – it's time to go! You will become a palaeontologist and go on an adventure looking for dinosaur fossils.

A good palaeontologist needs tools to do their job.

Walking boots

Brush

Spade

Magnifying glass

A palaeontologist is a scientist who studies what life on Earth was like before we humans came around. They go on excavations looking for fossils.

WHAT ARE FOSSILS?

A fossil is made when an animal or plant is **preserved** in rock. The hard parts, such as bone or shell, are left behind. They leave a shape in the rock for us to study.

Palaeontologists study lots of different types of fossil, from animals and plants to **bacteria**.

Palaeontologists are very careful with dinosaur fossils because they are millions of years old. They use brushes to carefully clean fossils and magnifying glasses to get a closer look.

Fossils are taken to laboratories to be cleaned and studied.

STEGOSAURUS

Plates

Spikes

Do you know what Stegosaurus looked like? Stegosaurus was very heavy with a spiky tail and big plates along its back.

8

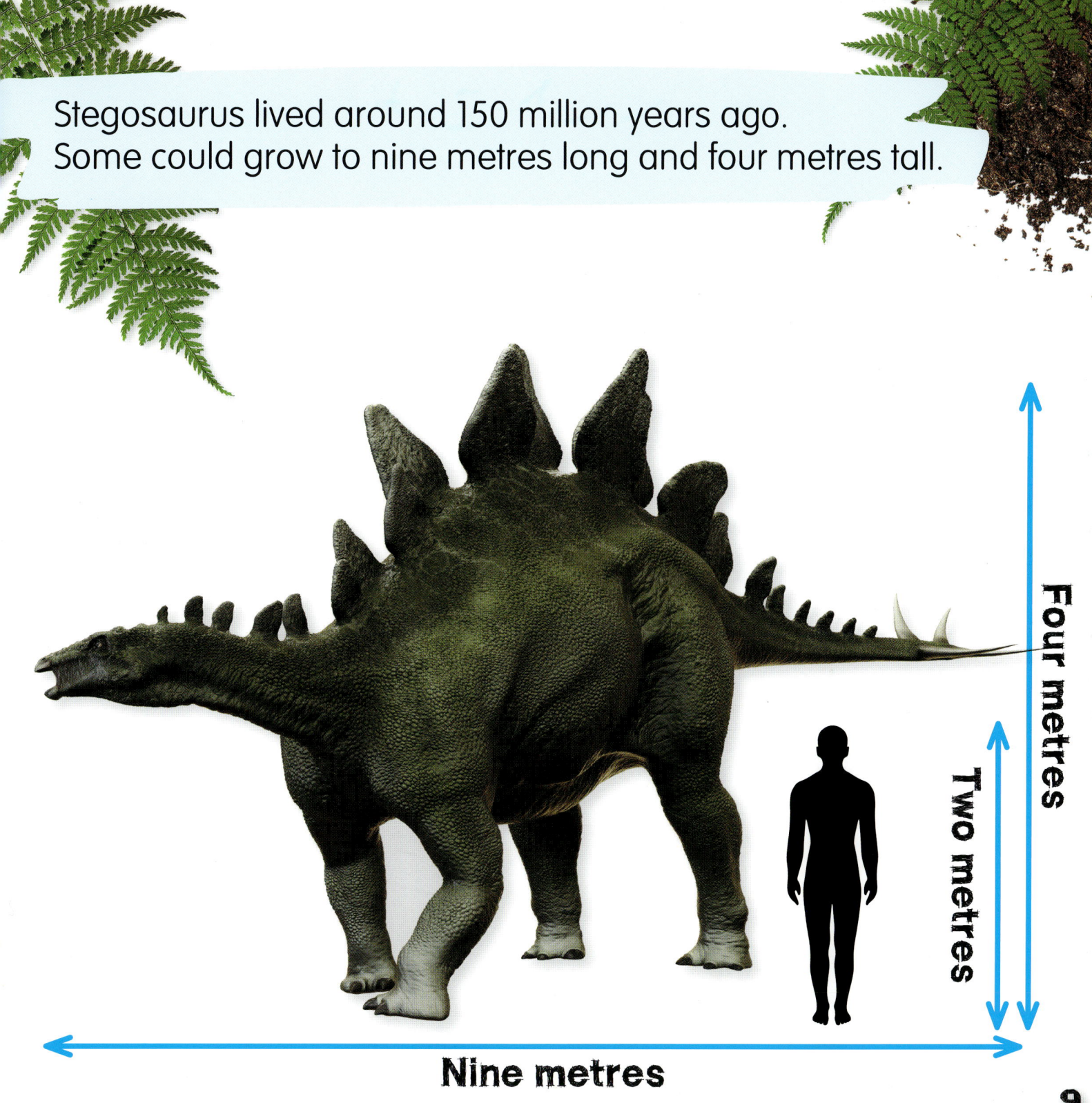

Stegosaurus lived around 150 million years ago.
Some could grow to nine metres long and four metres tall.

Four metres

Two metres

Nine metres

PALAEONTOLOGISTS OF THE PAST

Palaeontologist Othniel Marsh was confused when he discovered Stegosaurus fossils in 1877. He wasn't sure how Stegosaurus's plates lined up on its back.

Othniel Marsh

Marsh's drawing showed eight larger plates. Can you count all eight?

Sophie the Stegosaurus

In 2003, palaeontologist Bob Simon was digging for fossils when he found Sophie the Stegosaurus. This fossil has helped palaeontologists to learn a lot about Stegosaurus.

Sophie

LET'S DIG

It looks like people have already started digging here.

It's time to think about where to start our excavation. We need to find the right site. Palaeontologists look at special maps to find areas where the rock is very old.

It's a good idea to think about the **habitat** that Stegosaurus lived in. Palaeontologists believe that Stegosaurus lived in forests where North America is today.

Let's put on our walking boots and start excavating...

TINY TEETH

Is there a fossil in the ground? It needs to be gently removed so we can brush off the dirt and get a closer look.

Now it's clean, we can see it's a Stegosaurus skull. Look at the tiny teeth! Stegosaurus had 78 teeth that were the size of fingernails. These teeth were perfect for grinding down plants.

Stegosaurus skull

Stegosaurus was a herbivore. This must be why it liked to live in forests.

WHAT ARE THOSE?

Stegosaurus armour

Armour

You might be wondering what the massive plates on Stegosaurus's back were for. A lot of palaeontologists believe that the plates were hard like armour.

Some palaeontologists think that the plates on Stegosaurus's back helped Stegosaurus to find a **mate**. Stegosaurus with big plates could show them off.

ALL THE BETTER TO HIT YOU WITH

Can you see the spikes on Stegosaurus's tail? The four spikes were used as a weapon against **predators**.

Spikes

Can you count all the spikes?

Thagomizer

Stegosaurus would swing its tail to give predators a good whack! This type of spiked tail is called a thagomizer.

WHAT IF...

What if Stegosaurus was brightly coloured? If you picture Stegosaurus, you might imagine a big green dinosaur. But what if Stegosaurus was a different colour?

What colour do you think Stegosaurus was? Was Stegosaurus striped or spotted? Red or blue?

Sometimes there are things that fossils can't tell us. Palaeontologists don't know what colour Stegosaurus really was. Skin is soft and less likely to be preserved in a fossil than bones.

For now, we have to guess what Stegosaurus would have looked like if it had pretty patterns.

THINK AGAIN

Sometimes palaeontologists get things wrong at first. It was once believed that Stegosaurus had an extra brain near its bottom! Now palaeontologists know this is not true.

DO YOU MIND?!

END OF THE TREK

There's still a lot to discover as a palaeontologist. New fossils are being excavated and studied all the time. Maybe you could be the next person to discover a dinosaur as super as Stegosaurus!

GLOSSARY

bacteria   tiny living things, which are too small to see, that can cause diseases

excavations   careful removals of earth from an area in order to uncover buried remains or ruins

habitat   the natural home in which animals or plants live

herbivore   an animal that only eats plants

laboratories   rooms or buildings used by scientists to carry out experiments and research

mate   an animal that another animal has babies with

predators   animals that hunt other animals for food

preserved   kept in its original form

site   a place where something is

INDEX